MONOLOGUES
from
CHEKHOV

Translated by

Mason W. Cartwright

Dramaline Publications

Dramaline Publications
36-851 Palm View Road
Rancho Mirage, CA 92270
Phone 619/770-6076 Fax 619/770-4507

Library of Congress Cataloging-in-Publication Data

Chekhov, Anton Pavlovich, 1860-1904.
   [Plays. English. Selections.]
   Monologues from Chekhov / translated by Mason W. Cartwright.
      p.   cm.
   Selections from The Seagull, Uncle Vanya, The Three Sisters, and
The Cherry Orchard.
   ISBN 0-940669-03-X (alk. paper)
   1. Chekhov, Anton Pavlovich, 1860-1904—Translations into English.
I. Cartwright, Mason W. II. Title.
PG3456.A13C37   1995
891.72'3—de20   95-25799

This book is printed on 55# Glatfelter acid-free paper, a paper that meets the requirements of the American Standard of Permanence of paper for printed library material.

CONTENTS

TRANSLATOR'S NOTE

The following translations are taken from A. P. Chekhov, *Polnoe Sobraine Sochineii*, as published in 1903 by A. F. Marsha, Sta. Petersburg.

My goal was to contemporize Chekhov's speeches with an ear to their presentation by today's actors in the pursuit of their craft without unduly distorting or diminishing their power, meaning, and rhythm. Hopefully, that goal has been achieved.

MASON W. CARTWRIGHT

THE SEAGULL
(1896)

The action of the play transpires at the Sorin estate. On hand are Irina Nikolaevna (Mrs. Treplev), a self-centered, middle-aged actress, and her lover, Trigorin, a successful, hedonistic writer. Arkadina's son, Konstantin Treplev, desires to be a writer, an original writer of new forms, but his writings are naive and rife with confusing symbolism. Treplev is in love with—and wants to marry—Nina, the young daughter of a nearby landowner. Nina, young and impressionable, a naive, aspiring actress, is overwhelmed by the famous Trigorin and leaves with him as his new mistress. The play is fraught with other underlying character problems and conflicts. Sorin, Arkadina's older brother, regrets never marrying and becoming a writer. Masha, the daughter of Sorin's steward, had wanted to marry Treplev but instead married the poor, complaining schoolteacher Medvedenko, who is disillusioned because he cannot get Masha to accept her domestic responsibilities. Overcome by frustrations (the inability to conquer his craft, his mother's indifference, the shallowness of her art and Trigorin's, and Nina's rejections), Treplev ends his own life.

WOMEN:

Act One. Nina. A stage in the park of the Sorin estate.

On a stage constructed on the grounds of the estate, Nina reads the opening lines of Treplev's play, a work of symbols that is met with derision by his mother, who declares the play "depraved nonsense."

NINA

Men, women, lions, eagles, geese, fish in the sea, all life, all creatures invisible to the eye—all having gone through their sad life cycles—they are now extinct. A thousand centuries have lapsed on this planet without a single living thing . . . this moon has lit her lamp in vain. Now on this meadow no one awakes to the cry of cranes, to the sound of May beetles in the lime groves. All is cold, empty, terrible!

(*Pause.*) The bodies of all living creatures have all turned to dust; eternal matter has reduced them to stones, water, and clouds. But their souls have become one. I am the one soul of the world.

Yes . . . In me is the soul of Alexander the Great, Caesar, Shakespeare, Napoleon—the soul of the most insignificant worm. The instincts of animals, the consciousness of all humanity are joined in me. I remember all, everything . . . in me lives every other life.

(*Pause.*) I am lonely. I open my lips to speak once in a hundred years and my sad voice echoes unheard throughout the void. And you, you pale lights, you do not hear me either. The foul marsh gives you birth each morning and you dwell there till break of day . . . without thought, without will, without quiver of life. Fearing life will awake you, the devil, the father of eternal matter, controls your every moment as he does the atoms in stones and water; and you, like them, keep changing forever. In the whole universe, only the spirit remains constant and immutable. (*Pause.*) Like a prisoner cast into a deep, empty well, I don't know where I am or what awaits me. All is hidden from me, except for my struggle with the devil; a struggle I will win. Then spirit and matter will unite and the reign of Universal Will will follow. But this will only happen slowly, over a succession of millennia, and after the moon, the stars, the earth itself have turned to dust. Until that time—only horror. (*Pause. Two red spots appear against the background of the lake.*) Look! My mighty adversary the devil comes. I see his terrifying blood-red eyes.

Act Four. Nina. A drawing room in the Sorin house.

Two years earlier, Nina ran off with famous writer Trigorin and had a child by him, which perished at birth. Trigorin tired of her and returned to his old attachments. Turning to the stage, Nina's debut was less than auspicious. Now, on her way to an undistinguished theatrical engagement in a small city, Nina has stopped off to see Treplev, the young writer she deserted for Trigorin.

NINA

I was afraid you hated me. Night after night, I have the same dream—that you look at me but don't know me. If you only knew! From the time I got here, I've been walking by the lake. I've walked back and forth in front of your house many times, but I couldn't get up the nerve to see you. Let's sit down. (*They sit.*) It's nice and warm here. Cozy. The wind—hear it? It reminds me of a passage from Turgenev: "Lucky is a person on a night like this, who has a warm corner." I'm a seagull . . . no, no . . . (*She rubs her forehead.*) What was I thinking about? Oh, yes—Turgenev . . . "And may the Lord help all the homeless wanderers . . . " Never mind, it's nothing. (*She sobs.*) It's good, it gives me some relief . . . you realize I've gone two years without crying. Last night I went to the garden to see if our stage was still standing. And there it was. I cried then, for the first time in two years—what a relief. It was good for me. There, see— I'm crying now. (*She grasps him by the hand.*)

So, you've become a writer. You a writer, me an actress. We're caught in the whirlpool, you and I. When I was young, I was happy. I had a happy life. Every morning I woke up singing. I loved you and I dreamed of fame. Fame. Early tomorrow morning I'm off to Yelets, third-class with the peasants. And in Yelets, cultured businessmen will bother me with their foolishness. Life is sad.

Act Four. Nina. A drawing room in the Sorin estate.

In an act of contrition, Nina has returned after two years to confront Treplev before journeying to a small community to fulfill a theatrical commitment. Here she speaks of her descent to near oblivion with Trigorin, her acting, the realization that work is all.

NINA

You shouldn't say you kiss the ground I walk on. You should want to kill me. (*She bends over a table.*) I'm so tired. If I could only rest. (*She raises her head.*) I'm a seagull. No! I'm an actress. Yes. (*Hearing the laughter of Arkadina and Trigorin OFF, she listens, then runs to the door and peers through the keyhole.*)

So, he's here, too. (*She returns to Treplev.*) So? It's nothing. So what? He doesn't believe in theater. He laughed at my dreams continuously to the point I didn't believe in them either or believe in myself. Then there were the worries of love, jealously, constant fears for my baby. I became nothing, I acted without thinking. I didn't know what to do with my hands; I couldn't stand properly on stage or control my voice. You can't imagine what it's like to know you're acting badly.

I'm a seagull. No—that's not what I meant. Remember, remember when you shot a seagull? A man comes along and shoots a seagull just for the fun of it. A subject for a short story. No—I didn't mean that. (*She rubs her forehead.*)

What was I talking about? Oh yes, I was talking about the stage. I'm not like I used to be. Now I'm a real actress. I get caught up in my roles, overcome. On the stage I'm intoxicated, I feel beautiful up there. Since I've been here, I've been walking a lot; walking and thinking and feeling my mind and spirit getting stronger each day.

You know, Kostya, I've come to realize that for an actor or writer, the important thing isn't fame or money, it's knowing how to endure, how to bear your cross and have faith. Now that I have faith, it isn't so painful anymore, and I'm not afraid of life when I think of acting for a living.

Act Four. Nina. A drawing room in the Sorin Estate.

In her final speech, near the end of the play, Nina says farewell to Treplev, recalls simpler times, and recites lines from his play. She also states her enduring love for Trigorin, a reality that contributes ultimately to Trelpev's self-destruction.

NINA

(*Listening.*) Sh—I'm, going. Good-bye. When I become a great actress, come see me. Promise? But now . . . (*She takes his hand.*) I'm weak, I can hardly stand up. I need something to eat. (*Pause.*) So, she brought Trigorin along. Well, it doesn't matter. When you see him, don't tell him I was here. I love him, even more than I did before. It would make a good short story. I love him! Love him desperately, passionately. Remember how good it was before, Kostya? Remember? What a wonderful life it was . . . so warm and pure and happy! And what feelings we used to have—feelings like tender, elegant flowers. Do you remember? (*She recites.*) "Men and lions, eagles and partridges, geese, spiders, the silent fish swimming in the sea, starfishes and creatures invisible to the eye—life, all life, all life, all have lived and died and are now extinct. A thousand centuries have passed and the earth has not borne a single living thing, and the poor moon has lit her light in vain. Now on this meadow no one awakes to the sound of cranes, to the sound of May beetles in the lime groves." (*She embraces Treplev impulsively and runs out through the door.*)

Act Two. Arkadina. A croquet lawn on the Sorin estate.

Arkadina's vanity, egotism, her exaggerated sense of self-assurance are apparent in this speech to Masha.

ARKADINA

Stand up, stand next to me. (*They stand.*) There now—look. You're only twenty-two, and I'm almost twice your age. Let me ask you, who looks younger? And you know why? Because I'm working, I'm involved, I'm on the move constantly, while you stay in one place day after day. You're not living. And another thing, I have this rule: I never dwell on the future. Never. Never think about dying. What will be, will be. (*Pause.*) And I'm very particular about myself, too. As particular as an English noblewoman. My dear, as the saying goes, I keep myself up. I'm always well-dressed and my hair well-styled. You think I'd leave the house, even come into my garden looking sloppy? Never. The reason I look so good for my age is because I've never let myself go as so many women do. (*She paces up and down the lawn with her arms akimbo.*) There. See that? Light as a feather. I could play the part of a fifteen-year-old girl, right now. (*She takes up a book.*) Now, let's get on with the reading. It's my turn. Where were we? Here we are. "And it stands to reason that for society people to butter up novelists and lure them into their homes is just as dangerous for a grain merchant to breed rats in his storehouses. And yet, they come and play up to them. When a woman is out to get a novelist, she flatters him, does him all kinds of favors . . ."

Well, it may be like that in France, but not in Russia. We don't lay traps. Here women are usually in love with a writer before they set out to get him. Just look at Trigorin and me, for instance.

Act Three. Arkadina. The dining room in the Sorin estate.

As Arkadina and Trigorin prepare to depart the Sorin estate, Trigorin reveals his infatuation with Nina, a young, aspiring actress. Here, Arkadina, angered and threatened, expresses her feelings for him with dramatic importunity.

ARKADINA

Am I so old and ugly that you can talk to me like this about other women? (*She embraces and kisses him.*) You've lost your mind! (*She falls to her knees.*) You're my happiness, my joy, my life! (*Hugging his knees.*) If you leave me, even for an hour, I won't make it. I'll lose my mind, my wonderful, beautiful man. My master. (*She kisses his hands.*) You're everything to me, you crazy boy, everything! You think I'm going to let you go off and do something crazy? Never! (*She laughs.*) You're mine. Mine! (*Touching him.*) This forehead's mine, these eyes are mine. You're all mine! And you're so talented, gifted, the best of our writers, Russia's only hope. You write with such sincerity and freshness and humor, you can bring to light the depths of people and places with a single stroke of the pen. Your characters live! It's impossible to read you without being uplifted. You think I'm exaggerating? Flattering? No, never. You don't believe me? Just look in my eyes . . . go ahead, look . . . do you see a liar? Do you? I'm the only one who can truly appreciate you, who'll tell you the truth, my dear darling. You will come with me, won't you? You're not going to leave me, are you?

MEN:

Act One. Treplev. The park on the Sorin estate.

A stage has been erected in the park of the Sorin estate and a new work, written by Treplev and starring Nina, is to begin at moonrise. Here, an anxious Treplev speaks to his uncle, Sorin, regarding his mother's behavior. (Note: In the interest of greater duration, this speech may be coupled with the one that follows.)

TREPLEV

Mother is bored. (*He sits down beside his uncle.*) And jealous. She's against me and the play and the performance because Nina's in it and she isn't. She already hates the play and doesn't know a thing about it. And she's mad because, even on this tiny stage, Nina will be a hit and she won't. (*Looking at his watch.*) My mother—the mental case. Oh, she's talented, all right, no doubt about it—and intelligent. She can cry her eyes out over a book, reel off all of Nekrasov's poems from memory, and if someone's sick, she'll take care of him like an angel . . . but just try to praise Duse in front of her! Oh boy! Watch out! You can only praise mother, and write glowing reviews about her and rave about her performances in *The Lady with the Camellias* or *It's a Mad Life.* Out here in the country, where she's not getting praise all the time, she's bored and cross and everybody is her enemy, And she's superstitious, too—afraid of three candles burning and the number thirteen and things that. And she's stingy. I know for a fact she has seventy thousrubles in a bank in Odessa. But ask her for a loan and see what happens. She'll break down and cry like baby.

Act One. Treplev. The park on the Sorin Estate.

Treplev tells Sorin that his mother does not love him, that he is nothing more to her than a reminder of encroaching old age, reveals his contempt for the theater of the day.

TREPLEV

(*Tearing the petals from a flower.*) She loves me, she loves me not, she loves me, she loves me not, she loves me, she loves me not. (*He laughs.*) You see—Mother doesn't love me. Why should she? All I am is a twenty-five-year-old reminder that she's no longer a young woman. When I'm not around, she's only thirty-two; when I am, she's forty-three, and she hates me for it. And to make it worse, she knows I don't accept the theater. She loves the theater and thinks she's serving mankind and the sacred cause of art. As far as I'm concerned, the theater's stuck in the past. It's the same old stuff. The audience is looking through a fourth wall at an artificially lit set at artists who are supposed to have talent; so-called stars who are the guardians of a sacred art, depicting how people eat and drink and dress and love. And then they try to bring to shallow work some little, cozy, easy-to-grasp moral, suitable for home consumption. When they hand me the same old rehash time after boring time, that's when I run. Like de Maupassant did when he saw the Eiffel Tower because it would corrupt his mind.

Act One. Treplev. The park on the Sorin Estate.

Treplev, disgusted by the state of the theater, frustrated with his life as the insignificant son of a famous mother, reveals his feelings to his uncle, Sorin. (Note: if a monologue of greater duration is desired, this speech may be coupled with the one preceding.)

TREPLEV

What we need in the theater of today are new forms. If not, then we'd be better off without the theater. (*He notes his watch.*) I love my mother, I really do, but her rattle-brained life, her running around all over the place with that novelist, her name in the papers all the time—it wears me out. Sometimes I think I'd be much happier if my mother were just an ordinary person. Can you imagine, Uncle, a more desperate situation than this? We're usually surrounded by celebrities, actors, and writers—and in their midst, here I am . . . a nobody, someone they put up with only because I'm her son. Who am I? What am I? I left the university in my third year, "owing to circumstances," as they say. I'm not talented, I'm broke, and according to my passport, I am a petty bourgeois from Kiev. Like my father was, you know, even though he was a famous actor, too. Usually, when actors and writers who visited my mother paid attention to me, I felt like they thought I was nothing. I knew what they were thinking, and I can't tell you how deeply it hurt.

Act Four. Treplev. A drawing room in the Sorin estate.

Two years earlier, Nina ran off with the famous writer Trigorin, who proved to be a spineless roué. Here, Treplev updates Dr. Dorn relative to her adventures, and exposes his enduring attachment to his beloved Nina.

TREPLEV

Of course, you know she ran away with Trigorin. And had his baby and the baby died. Then Trigorin got tired of her and went back to his old attachments, as you might expect. In fact, he'd never given them up. He'd been looking back and forth between Nina and his old loves in keeping with his weak character. From what I've heard, Nina's life has been a disaster. Her stage career even worse, it seems. She made her debut at a little resort near Moscow, then went on a tour of the provinces. I never let her out of my sight in those days, and wherever she appeared, I followed. She tried to play all the big parts, but her acting was crude and tasteless and full of ranting and stiff gestures. Oh, there were moments, of course. Every now and then she cried well, sometimes her dying scenes were effective. She had some talent, I suppose, but it was hard to tell. I saw her, but she wouldn't see me. Her maid wouldn't let me into her room. I knew how she felt, so I didn't push it. (*Pause.*) What else can I tell you? After I came home, I got some letters from her that were warm, intelligent, and provocative, and she didn't complain. But I could tell she was very unhappy because there was tension in every line. You could tell she was upset. She kept signing her letters "The Seagull." And she kept referring to herself as a seagull, like the miller in *The Mermaid* kept calling himself a raven. She's here now, you know? In town, at the inn. She's been here for about five days. I've tried to see her, and Masha has tried, too. But she won't see anyone.

Act Four. Treplev. A drawing room in the Sorin estate.

Treplev agonizes over his writing.

TREPLEV

(*At his desk, he peruses what he has written.*) I've talked a lot about new forms, but I'm afraid by my little writings becoming more conventional. (*He reads.*) "The poster on the fence proclaimed a white face framed by dark hair . . . " "Proclaimed, framed." No no! That's awful! (*He crosses out.*) I think I'll start where the hero is awakened by the rain, and cut the rest. The description of the moonlit evening is way too long and too cute. This would be easy for Trigorin—he'd have the moonlit night worked out in a minute by having the broken neck of a bottle glistening, and the shadow of the mill wheel looming darker and darker. Easy for him. But look what I've got. "Tremulous light, the soft glimmer of stars, faraway sounds of a piano fading off in the calm, fragrant air." Awful! (*Pause.*) More and more, I'm coming to the conclusion that it's not a matter of old or new forms. I think the important thing is to forget about forms and allow what you feel to come pouring straight from your heart to the paper.

Act Two. Trigorin. The lawn on the Sorin estate.

*Nina, an aspiring actress, young and impressionable, is over-
whelmed by the famous writerTrigorin. Here, during their first en-
counter, Trigorin tells her of his obsessivenesss, his early self-
doubts. We learn of his frustrations, his feelings of shallowness
because he doesn't rise above the trivial and deal with the great
social themes.*

TRIGORIN

(*Shrugging his shoulders.*) Hmm . . . you speak of fame, happiness,
my brilliant and exciting life. Fine words. But—excuse me for saying
so—these words are like jelly to me, which I never eat. But thanks
anyway, you're very young and very kind. (*He notes his watch.*)
Excuse me, I've got to write.   (*He takes a step, then holds up with a
laugh.*) No. You've hit a nerve, and I'm starting to get excited and a
little angry. So, all right, let's talk about my wonderful, brilliant life.
Now, let's see . . . where shall we begin? (*A pause for thought.*)

You know how some people become obsessed with something,
like the moon, for instance? Well, I guess you might say writing is
my moon. All I think about night and day is writing—I must write, I
must write, I must! And as soon as I finish one story, I have to start
another, and then another and another. It never ends. I ask you,
what's so beautiful and brilliant about that, eh? It's a crazy and
lonely way to live. Here I am, excited, talking to you, but at the same
time I can't get my mind off my work, the story that's waiting for me
in my room. I see that cloud up there and I see it as a grand piano and
I make a mental note of it for my story—"A cloud that looked like a
grand piano floated by." I smell the heliotrope, and I capture it in my
mind so I can remember it and use it for a description of a summer
evening. I catch myself listening to everything I say, and everything

you say, too, and I lock up all the words and phrases in my literary storehouse. Who knows when they might come in handy?

When I finish working, I go to the theater or go fishing to try to forget about writing, but I can't because already some new subject, some new story is starting to roll around like a cannonball in my head. So I hurry back to my desk and write, write, write! And that's the way it is, always. I can't get away from myself. I feel like I'm consuming my own life. To make honey to give away to someone I don't know, I steal the pollen from my best flowers, pick them, and then trample their roots.

You think I've lost my mind? Do you? You think my friends treat me like a normal person? "What are you writing now?" they ask. "What's you next story?" It's always the same. They give me attention, they flatter me. But—between you and me—I think it's phony. They're deceiving me, like you do a sick person. I'm afraid sometime they're going to grab me from behind and cart me off to the asylum like they did the crazy man in Gogol.

When I was starting out, during my best years, writing was nothing but sheer agony. A beginning writer, especially if he's unlucky, feels awkward and unwanted. His nerves are on edge, near the breaking point, and he can't stay away from people connected with art and where he's unrecognized, unnoticed, and so shy he can't look anyone in the eye—like a compulsive gambler without any money.

Even though I don't know my readers, I picture them as skeptical, unfriendly critics. I used to be scared to death of theater audiences, terrified. And when I had a new play produced, it seemed like all the dark-haired people in the audience were out to get me and the blondes couldn't give a damn less. It was agony! Torture!

I do find pleasure when I'm writing, though. And when I'm reading proofs. But after it's published, I hate it and wish I'd never written it. I feel angry, irritable, rotten. Like it was all a mistake. (*He laughs.*) Then the public reads it, and you hear, "Ah, yes, very clever, he's gifted . . . but he's no Tolstoy." Or, "Very good, but Turgenev's *Fathers and Children* is better. To my dying day I'll be clever and gifted—nothing more. After I'm dead, my friends will visit my grave and say, "Here lies Trigorin. A good writer, but he couldn't touch Turgenev." (*Pause.*)

I dislike myself as a writer, I've never been pleased with my work. Most of the time I'm in a daze and don't know what I'm writing. I love water, trees, the sky—I have a feeling for nature, a passion for it and it inspires me to write. But I'm more than a landscape painter—I'm a citizen who loves Russia and its people, and if I'm really a writer, I should be writing about the people and their sufferings, about their future, about science and learning, and the rights of man. I write everything hastily with angry people pushing from all sides. And I run from one side to the other like a fox being chased by hounds. And life and science keep striding ahead, onward and forward, while I keep falling behind, always a little too late, like a peasant missing a train. In the final analysis, I think I'm nothing more than a landscape writer. Everything else I write is phony to the core.

UNCLE VANYA
(1897)

Old Serebryakov has returned with his young wife, Elena, to the Serebryakov estate and has thrown things into disorder. The brother of Serebryakov's first wife, Uncle Vanya, has lost interest in maintaining the estate and is disenchanted by Serebryakov's egotistical complaining and has found him to be a fraudulent, demanding nuisance. He is also frustrated by his unreturned love for Elena. Sonia, Serebryakov's daughter by his first wife, is deeply in love with Dr. Astroff and is distressed because he does not reciprocate due to the fact that he is infatuated with Elena. This distraction leaves her depleted, unable to cope with the responsibilities of the estate. Serebryakov, Sonia, Elena, and Astroff lead useless, disorderly lives while feeding on the energies of others. Matters are brought to a head when Serebryakov announces that he plans to sell the estate, an act that would leave Vanya, Sonia, and Vanya's mother destitute. But disaster is averted when Elena, fearful of her passion for Astroff, persuades Serebryakov to leave. After their departure, Vanya, Sonia, and Astroff return to old patterns: Vanya and Sonia to manage the estate, Astroff to doctoring and ecology, all resolved to lives of suffering and frustration.

WOMEN:

Act One. Elena. A garden on the Serebryakov estate.

Dr. Astroff has just exited after a lengthy speech regarding man's destructiveness, leaving Elena, the young wife of professor Serebryakov, and Vanya alone in the garden. When Vanya alludes to her bored expression, Elena responds with an echo of Astroff's philosophy and favorable observations with respect to his persona.

ELENA

Yes, living is an effort, and boring, too. Everybody chides my husband, and they all look at me with such pity. "Oh, the poor girl, married to an old man." All this concern for me, oh, how well I can understand it. Just like Astroff was saying a minute ago: all of you carelessly destroying the forests, and soon there won't be anything left on this Earth. Just like you're carelessly destroying mankind, and soon, thanks to you, there won't be loyalty or purity or the capacity for self-sacrifice left, either. Why can't you ignore women who don't belong to you? Because—the doctor's right—there's a destructive demon inside all of you. You don't give a damn for nature, for women, or even for each other. (*Pause.*) The doctor looks tired and tense. What a handsome face. You can see Sonia's attracted to him—in love with him. I can see why. He's been here three times since I arrived, but my shyness keeps me from talking to him like I should. In fact, I haven't been very kind. He must think I'm awful.

You and I are such good friends, Vanya . . . probably because we're such boring, tiresome people.

Act Two. Elena. The dining room in the Serebryakov house.

Sonia, frustrated by her unreturned love for Astroff, is told by Elena that the doctor's quality is genius. In this speech, she voices a recurring philosophy in Chekhov—futurism.

ELENA

It isn't forestry or medicine, my dear. No—it's his genius. And you know what genius means, don't you? It means courage, a free mind, broad vision. When he plants a tree, he is already imagining what it will be like in a thousand years; he envisions the beginnings of happiness for mankind. People like Astroff are rare birds who must be given love. All right, so he drinks, so he's occasionally rude, so what? A genius in Russia can't be expected to be a saint. And think of the kind of life he has: muddy, nearly impassable roads, freezing weather, great distances, wild, crude peasants, poverty and sickness everywhere. A person who works in this kind of situation day after day and reaches forty can't be expected to be perfect and sober. (*Pause.*) With everything in me I wish you the very best, you deserve happiness. I'm a boring, nothing person . . . in my music, in my husband's house, in my love affairs. In fact, wherever you look I'm nothing but an incidental character. To be perfectly honest, Sonia, when you stop to think about it, I'm a very, very unhappy woman. (*She paces back and forth.*) There's no happiness for me in this world. None!

Act Three. Elena. The living room in the Serebryakov house.

Rather than live with uncertainty, Sonia has agreed to allow Elena to find out if Dr. Astroff loves her. In the following monologue, Elena discloses her lusting feelings, her contrition for them.

ELENA

There's nothing worse than knowing someone else's secret and not being able to help. (*Deliberating.*) He's doesn't love her, that's obvious. But why shouldn't he marry her? She's not pretty, but she'd be a perfect wife for a country doctor his age. And she's smart, too, and kind . . . pure. No, that isn't it . . . (*Pause.*)

I can understand how she feels. Here she is stuck out here with all these gray people with their petty talk who just eat, drink, and sleep and then—every now and then like a bright light in the darkness—he walks in . . . handsome, intelligent, charming, totally different from the others. It's easy to forget yourself and be charmed by someone like him. I believe I'm a little fascinated myself. Yes, I'm bored without him. Uncle Vanya says I'm a bit of a nymph. "Just once in your life, let yourself go." Well . . . maybe I should. To fly off, free as a bird, away from all your sleepy faces, your constant jabbering, to forget that any of you ever existed in the world. But I can't. I'm too cowardly, too shy. I'd never get it off my conscience. He comes here every day, and I can guess why, and I already feel guilty.

I'm ready to fall on my knees in front of Sonia and cry and beg her to forgive me.

Act Three. Sonia. The living room in the Serebryakov house.

Frustrations stemming from inner conflicts, repressed emotions, and unrequited love have resulted in Sonia and Elena lapsing into a state of ennui. Here, Sonia expresses these feelings as well as distress for her unattractiveness, and Astroff's indifference.

SONIA

Don't stay bored, dear. (*She laughs.*) You're bored, you don't know what to do with yourself, and boredom and idleness are infectious. Just look around. Here's Uncle Vanya following you around like he's your shadow. And I stop what I'm doing and come in here and talk. I'm so lazy I don't know what to do! And we hardly ever used to see Dr. Astroff at all, maybe once a month. But now, because of you, he's out here every day instead of taking care of his forests and his medicine. You must be a witch. (*She notes herself in the mirror.*) I'm homely, no getting around it. (*Pause.*) What? I have pretty hair? That's what they always tell a homely woman. "You have pretty hair, nice eyes." You know, I've been in love with Dr. Michail Lvovitch for six years. I love him more than my own mother. Every waking moment I hear the sound of his voice, feel the touch of his hand. I keep watching the door, hoping he'll come in. Here, for instance, I come to you just so I can talk about him. He's out here every day now, but he doesn't give me a tumble. It's killing me! Tearing me up inside! I don't have any home anymore, none! (*Desperately.*) God, give me strength! I was awake all night—praying. I approach him repeatedly, talk to him, looking into his eyes . . . I have no pride. I can't control myself. Yesterday I lost control completely and told Uncle Vanya I love him. All the servants know it. Everybody knows! But he doesn't know I'm alive.

Act Four. Sonia. Uncle Vanya's room.

Elena, Serebryakov, and Astroff have departed, leaving Sonia and Uncle Vanya to a life of plodding desolation. Here, in the play's concluding speech, Sonia states her resolve, speaks of the sweet release she and Uncle Vanya will find in death.

SONIA

Well, what can you do? Life goes on! (*Pause.*) We'll keep on living, Uncle Vanya, through a long succession of everlasting nights and days, enduring whatever the fates have in store. We shall work for others now and in our old age, never knowing rest and peace. And when our time comes, we'll die without complaining. And beyond the grave we will say we have suffered, and wept, and that our life was hard and bitter, and God will take pity on us. And then, Uncle Vanya, we shall see a life that is bright and beautiful and fine, and we'll look back on our present misfortunes with a feeling of tenderness and smile. And we'll be at peace. I believe this, Uncle, I really do, fervently, passionately. (*In a tired voice.*) We shall find peace! And we shall hear the angels, and see the whole sky shining like diamonds. We shall see all our suffering, all the evils of this life drowned in a mercy that will fill the whole world, and then our life will become quiet and gentle as a caress. I believe this. I believe! Poor Uncle Vanya, you're crying. (*Through tears.*) You've never had any happiness in your life, but wait, just wait, Uncle Vanya, you will. We shall rest. We shall rest. We shall rest!

MEN:

Act One. Astroff. A garden on the Serebryakov estate.

Dr. Astroff, a man frustrated by life, tells nurse Marina his profession is an aging encumbrance, speaks to her of the futility of his labors.

ASTROFF

In just ten years I've become a different person. And you know the reason? Because I've been working too hard, that's why. From morning to night without letup, always on the go. And at night I lie under the bedcovers scared to death I'm going to get called out to see a patient. For as long as we've know each other, I've never had a single day off, not one! No wonder I'm looking old. And life itself is boring, stupid, sordid. It drags you down, a life like this. All day long you're surrounded by odd people, everywhere you look, one odd person after the other. After a while, after two or three years—you become odd, too, without even knowing it. You can't help it. (*He twists his long mustache.*)

   Look at this huge, stupid mustache I've grown, nurse. I've become strange, too. At least, thank God, I haven't become stupid yet. I've still got my mind. Although it seems like my feelings are gone. I don't want anything, I don't need anything, I don't love anymore. Except you, maybe, maybe you're the one I love. (*He kisses her hand.*) When I was a little boy, I had a nurse like you. (*Pause.*) The third week of Lent I went to Malitskoye because they had an epidemic—typhus. Sick people were scattered all over their huts lying in the middle of mud and grime and rotten smells with the calves next to them and pigs running all over the place, too. I worked all day without sitting down once, without taking a bite to eat, and when I got home, they wouldn't give me a minute's peace. They brought in a railroad switchman, and while I was operating, he up and died on me under the chloroform. Then—when I least needed it—my feelings came back and tortured me with guilt and made me feel like I'd killed the man on purpose! I sat down and closed my eyes—like this—and thought: will those who live after us over the next two or three hundred years, the ones we're blazing a trail for, will they have a good word for us? Why, nurse, they won't even remember.

Act Two. Serebryakov. A dining room in the Serebryakov house.

The professor begins his speech by placing himself in the same league as Turgenev, an irony in view of the fact that Serebryakov is an intellectual fraud. He then lapses into his usual pattern of complaining and pomposity, carping to his young bride, Elena, regarding his ill and age, the futility of life among plebeians.

SEREBRYAKOV

I wonder why it's so hard for me to breathe? They say that Turgenev's angina came from his gout. I think it's the same with me. Damn old age! I hate it! To hell with it! Now that I'm old, I can't stand myself anymore. And you, you must detest the sight of me. And you should. I'm no fool, you know—I understand. You, a young, healthy, beautiful woman with your life in front of you with an old man like me, a living corpse. Well . . . don't think I don't know how you feel, because I do. It's foolish I'm still alive. But you won't have to wait long, you'll all be free soon enough because I'm not going to be around much longer. It looks like, because of me, everyone is getting weary, bored, is destroying their own youth, while I'm the only one who's enjoying life, who's satisfied. Yes! (*Pause.*)

All right, I'll be quiet, if that's what you want. Funny—whenever Vanya Voynitsky or that idiot mother of his talks your head off, then it's all right, everyone listens. But if I so much as open my mouth, everybody gets depressed. It's like they hate the sound of my voice. All right, say I am detestable, an egotist, a despot—doesn't my age give me the right to be a little self-centered? Maybe I deserve it. Isn't that possible, don't I have the right to a peaceful old age and some respect? You work your whole life to become a scholar, to get used to your own study, to the lecture hall, and your esteemed colleagues. Then suddenly, for no reason, you wind up rotting in this tomb with stupid people, listening everyday to their banal gibberish! I want to live! I love success, fame! I love making an impact on the world, and—here I am, living in exile! Here I am, an old man yearning for the past, seeing others become famous, fearing death. I can't stand it! I don't have the strength! And they won't even forgive me for being old.

Act One. Voynitsky. A garden on the Serebryakov estate.

Professor Serebryakov's return to the estate with his young bride, Elena, has caused Uncle Vanya (Voynitsky) to lose interest in managing the property. He has come to see through the professor and now views him as an untalented, arrogant, complaining bore. Here he voices his feelings and—with thinly veiled jealously due to the fact he is smitten with Elena—marvels at Serebryakov's success with women.

VOYNITSKY

I've nothing new to tell. It's the same old story. I'm still the same, except maybe worse because I've become lazy and don't do anything but fret around like a grouch. And my mother sits around raving about the emancipation of women. She's got one eye on the grave and one in her books of learning for a way to a new life. And the professor, like always, sits in his study, writing from morning till night.

> "With furrowed brow and toiling brain
> We write our epic odes,
> But neither we nor they will ever hear
> A bit of praise no matter what we write."

I feel sorry for the paper he writes on. He'd be better off writing his autobiography. Oh, what a subject that would be. A retired professor, get it, this dried up old mackerel with gout, rheumatism, and migraine with a liver swollen with jealously and envy—this well-educated, smoked fish living on his first wife's estate against his will because he hasn't got the money to live in town.

He's always endlessly complaining about his misfortunes, although, in fact, he's damned lucky. (*Nervously.*) How lucky can you get? He's nothing but the son of a common sexton, educated at a church school. He picked up degrees at a university and got a professorship and became this important person because he married a senator's daughter. All of this really doesn't mean anything, but just the same . . . here we have a person who for twenty-five years has lectured and written about art and who doesn't know a thing about it. For twenty-five years he's been writing and lecturing what intelligent people have known for years and what stupid people have no interest in. To be blunt, for twenty-five years he's been pouring from one empty pot to another. And at the same time what monumental conceit! What arrogance! What pretensions! Here he is retired and not one single living soul knows who he is. He's a complete unknown! For twenty-five years the man has been working in someone else's place. And look at him. He stalks around like a demigod! And I envy him! He's such a success with women! No Don Juan has ever done better! My own sister, his first wife, a beautiful, gentle woman, pure as the blue sky, noble and generous, who had more admirers than he had students—she loved him as only angels can love those who are as pure and beautiful as they. And my own mother, his mother-in-law, she still worships him with reverent awe. And his second wife, beautiful, intelligent—you just saw her—married him when he was already old and gave him her youth, her beauty, her freedom, her special radiance. And for what? Why?

Act Two. Voynitsky. The dining room in the Serebryakov house.

*After the scene with Elena, Uncle Vanya (Voynitsky) expresses his
unrequited love for the young woman, regrets for squandered oppor-
tunities, disdain for the fraudulent Serebryakov.*

VOYNITSKY

She's gone. (*Pause.*) Ten years ago I used to meet her at my sister's.
She was seventeen, and I was thirty-seven. Why didn't I fall in love
with her then and ask her to marry me? It was possible. She'd be my
wife now . . . yes. Now, during a thunderstorm, she'd be frightened
and I'd hold her in my arms and whisper, "Don't be afraid, I'm right
here." What a beautiful thought; I smile when I think about it. But
God, wait a minute, I'm getting all mixed up. Why am I old? Why
doesn't she understand me? Her conversation, her idle moralizing,
her silly, aimless thoughts about the end of the world—I hate it!
(*Pause.*)

How many ways I've been deceived! I used to worship the professor, the pitiful, gouty old fraud—I worked like an ox for him.
Sonia and I were like tight-fisted peasants squeezing every last drop
out of this place, driving hard bargains over vegetable oil and peas
and cottage cheese, scrimping and cutting corners so we could send
thousands of rubles to him. I was proud of his scholarship, I lived
and breathed the man, and everything he wrote and said I thought
was inspired by genius. God! Now look. Here he is, retired, and now
you can see through his entire life. After he's dead, his work will be
forgotten. He's a complete unknown! Nothing! Have I ever been deceived. What a fool I've been. Stupid!

Act Three. Voynitsky. The living room in the Serebryakov house.

Even though the estate is legally his daughter's, Serebryakov has selfishly suggested it be sold and the proceeds used to support him in his declining years. His proposal triggers a tirade by Vanya, during which he vents his anger and frustrations toward the ungrateful pedagogue.

VOYNITSKY

So, you'll sell the estate, huh? Great! A brilliant idea! And just where does that leave mother and me? And what about Sonia? It's clear I haven't had a drop of common sense till now. I guess I've been stupid. I always thought the estate belonged to Sonia. My father bought this place as a dowry for my sister. I guess I've been naive up till now. I didn't know we were going by Turkish law here. I thought this was Russia! I thought the estate passed from my sister to Sonia.

This is incredible, absolutely incredible! Either I've lost my mind or . . . this estate was bought, at the prices at the time, for ninety-five thousand rubles. My father paid seventy thousand down, leaving a mortgage of twenty-five thousand. Now—listen carefully . . . this estate would have never been bought if I hadn't given up my inheritance in favor of my sister, whom I loved dearly. Not only that, I worked like an ox for ten years and paid off the entire debt! The only reason this estate is free and clear is because of my efforts. And now, now that I'm old, the want to toss me out on my neck! For twenty-five years I've been running this estate, working like a dog, sending you money like a good manager. And what have I gotten for it? Nothing! You haven't even thanked me once! And all these years, even now, all I've been getting from you is a salary of five hundred rubles a year. A beggar's wages! And not once did you think of giving me even one more ruble. For twenty-five years, my mother and I have been living like moles here, and all the time all you were thinking of was you! Every day we talked about you and your work, we were proud of you, we pronounced you name with reverence, spent our nights reading your books and journals, which now I hate! We put you on a pedestal, we knew all your articles by heart. But now my eyes have been opened! I can see everything clearly now. You write about art—but you don't understand a single thing about it. All your works, which I used to love, aren't worth a damn! You've fooled all of us! (*Blocking Serebryakov's way.*) Wait! I haven't finished! You've wasted my life! Thanks to you, I've never really lived, you've destroyed the best years of my life! You are my worst enemy!

THE CHERRY ORCHARD
(1903–1904)

While Chekhov alluded to *The Cherry Orchard* as a comedy, its view of social change and tragic loss underpin the work with great seriousness, delicately posturing it between humor and pathos. The Ranevskayas are an aristocratic, feckless lot who have frittered away their lives and fortunes and are so desperately in need of funds that they are confronted with the necessity of selling off the cherry orchard on the family estate. While each realizes the necessity of selling the orchard, they procrastinate in doing so because it represents a carefree, bygone time when life was happy and free from impending social change. To Lyubov Andreevna, owner of the estate, the orchard symbolizes a time of youth and innocence, when she was secure with a husband and son. To Gayeff, her brother, a time when he could be concerned with being a carefree gentleman farmer, concerned primarily with his billiard game rather than financial realities. The characters of the play relate comically because each sees clearly the impracticality of the others while having no sense of his own folly. They attempt to adjust to a new Russian society but, comically and sadly, they remain curious anachronisms. Finally, when the estate is sold, the family moves off to new lives where, undoubtedly, the will continue to live extravagant, ludicrous, outmoded lives.

WOMEN:

Act One. Anya. The nursery on the Ranevskaya estate.

Anya, Lyubov Andreevna's teenage daughter, tells her stepsister Varya of the hardships of living in Paris, speaks of her mother's profligate ways.

ANYA

I'm home! Thank God! Tomorrow I'm getting up early and running through the orchard. If I could only get some sleep. I didn't sleep a wink on the train for worrying. You've got no idea what an awful time I've had. The week we left, just before Easter, it was freezing cold. And Charlotta never stopped talking and doing her stupid magic tricks all the way there. And when we finally got to Paris, it was snowing and cold. And I don't know much French; that didn't make it any easier. Mama was living on the fifth floor, and when I got there, I had to walk up. She was entertaining some French people, some women, and this old priest with a little book. The room was filled with smoke and not a bit cozy, and I felt so sorry for Mama I took her in my arms and held her tight and didn't let go. Afterward, Mama was gentle and sweet to me and kept on crying. She'd already sold her summer place near Menton and she was broke. I was, too. I didn't have a kopeck. We had to scrape together train fare to get home. Mama just can't seem to understand it. When we eat in the station restaurants, she orders the most expensive things and tips the waiters each a ruble. And Charlotta and Yasha were just as extravagant. Yasha's Mama's servant, you know . . . she brought him along with us. It was simply terrible!

Act Two. Lyubov Andreevna. A field.

A contrite Lyubov Andreevna speaks of her troubled life.

LYUBOV ANDREEVNA

Oh, my sins. I've always thrown money away impulsively, like a crazy woman, and then I married a man who did nothing but run up debts. And he drank himself to death, loved alcohol. And then—then I fell in love with another man and started living with him. And just then came my first punishment, a cruel blow. My little boy, my beloved Grisha was drowned right here—in this very river! I ran blindly, out of control, never wanting to come back—to see this river again! I just closed my eyes and ran, not knowing who I was or what I was doing, and *he* followed me, the cruel brute!

When he fell ill near Menton, I bought a villa there, and for three years I nursed him night and day. He wore me out completely, my soul dried up. Then last year, after I was forced to sell the villa to pay our debts, I went to Paris, where he robbed me and left me for another woman. I tried to commit suicide. It was all so foolish and degrading.

Then suddenly, I felt this overpowering urge to return to Russia, to my home and my land and my little girl. (*She brushes away tears.*) Oh God, dear God in heaven, be kind, please forgive me for my sins! (*She removes a telegram from her pocket.*) I got this telegram from Paris today. He's begging me to come back. (*She rips up the telegram.*)

Act Three. Lyubov Andreevna. A drawing room.

Trofimov, a student and forward-thinking intellectual, is also a naively smug pedant. He sees the cherry orchard and members of the Ranevskaya family as connections with the socially decadent past and is harshly vocal regarding his beliefs. When he implores the fretting Lyubov Andreevna to "face the truth," his remark triggers this multi-layered outpouring.

LYUBOV ANDREEVNA

What truth? You seem to be able to see what's true and what isn'., But not me. I see nothing. You're so confident, finding answers to all the important problems it seems. But be honest, isn't this because you're young and not old enough for any of your problems to have caused you any real suffering? You look to the future so boldly, you don't foresee anything terrible happening. But let me ask you, isn't this because you're too young to know what life's all about?

All right, you're bolder, more honest, deeper than we are. But please, show some understanding to our side of it, show some compassion for my feelings! Remember, I was born here, my father and mother lived here, my grandparents. I love this house. Without the cherry orchard, my life would be meaningless, and if it's sold, they might as well sell me with it. My son was drowned here, you know. (*She weeps.*) Please have pity on me, my friend. (*As she takes out her handkerchief, a telegram falls to the floor.*)

You just can't imagine what I've gone through today; my heart's sick. There's so much noise here, and it upsets me so it causes me to shake. But I can't go to my room. It's too frightening and lonely up there. Please don't condemn me, Petya, because I love you like a son, and I'd gladly let my Anya marry you, I swear, but you've got to buckle down and finish your studies. It's so strange how you do nothing, let fate toss you this way and that. It's the truth, isn't it? And you should do something about your beard. Train it properly. (*She laughs.*) Oh, you're so funny! (*Trofimov picks up the telegram.*)

It's a telegram from my crazy man in Paris. I get one every day. He's sick and in trouble again and he wants me to forgive him and come back to Paris and take care of him. I can see by the look on your face you disapprove. But think about it—what else can I do? After all, the man is sick and alone and unhappy. He needs someone around to keep an eye on him and to see he gets his medicine on time. Then—why try to hide it—I love him. I really do. I love him, I love him. Even though he's a millstone dragging me down, I love my millstone and can't live without it. Don't think badly of me, Petya, please. Don't say anything, don't speak.

MEN:

Act One. Gayev. The nursery of the Ranevskaya estate.

As a means of saving the day, it has been practically suggested that the cherry orchard be divided and sold off for summer homesites. But Lyubov Andreevna and brother Gayev are resisting this notion on foolish emotional grounds, and in this speech to Varya and Anya, Gayev typically proposes a fanciful scheme for raising money to save the estate.

GAYEV

When a lot of remedies are prescribed for a disease, it means there's no cure for it. I keep racking my brain for a remedy, and I've come up with a lot of them, which means, of course, I don't have a clue. It would be nice to inherit money, or marry off Anya to a rich man, or go to Yaroslavl and try our luck with our dear aunt, the countess. She's rich. But she doesn't give a damn for us. She resents the fact that my sister married a lawyer instead of nobility. (*Anya appears in the doorway.*) She may have not married into nobility, and maybe she's led a less than godly life, but she's a good, kind, wonderful person—and I love her very much. But still, you can't excuse—even though she's gone through a lot—you can't excuse her immoral behavior. (*He notices Anya in the doorway, is embarrassed, shifts the subject.*)

My little darling. My dear child, you're just not my niece, you're my angel, my everything. Believe me. (*Pause.*) Anya, my little darling, I didn't see you standing there. Come in. (*Anya enters. He kisses her hands and face.*) I'm sorry you heard what I said about your dear mother. It's terrible, terrible! God in heaven! And that foolish speech I made today at the bookcase . . . silly! I'll keep quiet. (*He kisses Anya's and Varya's hands.*)

But there's one thing I should mention. I was at the district court on Thursday and I talked to some people about our problem and it looks as though we might be able to get a loan to pay the interest. I'm going back on Tuesday and talk to them again. And your mother's going to talk to Lopakhin. He won't turn her down. And after you've rested, you'll go see your great aunt, the countess, in Yaroslavl. This way we'll be attacking the problem from all sides— we can't miss.

I'm sure we'll pay off the interest. I give you my word of honor, I'll swear on anything you want, this estate will not be sold! (*Excitedly.*) I swear on my own happiness! Here's my hand on it. You can call me a worthless scoundrel if I let this estate come up for auction. I'd die before I'd let it happen.

Act Two. Trofimov. A field.

Trofimov, a student, speaks of the folly of man's pride, the ignorance of Russia's so-called intelligentsia, inhuman realities that abound in his homeland.

TROFIMOV

We talked a lot yesterday and didn't settle a thing. When you talk about man's pride, you're referring to the mystical, spiritual side of him. Maybe from that point of view, you're right . . . maybe. But if you sort out the whole thing without emotion, look at it clearly, then what's to be proud of when you realize what a poor psychological specimen man is and how most of the human race is brutal, stupid, and profoundly unhappy? It's high time we stop admiring ourselves. The only thing to do is work. Humanity marches on, perfecting itself. All the things that are incomprehensible to us now will one day be commonplace if we apply ourselves and work and do all we can for those who seek the truth.

Today in Russia, very few people really work. All the educated people I know—most of them, anyway—are lazy and passive. They don't know what it is to work. They have the nerve to call themselves the intelligentsia while they talk down to their servants and treat the peasants like animals. Some students! They're lazy, they read pap, talk about science, and when it comes to art—they don't know a damned thing about it. These "serious" little people with grim faces. While they discuss and philosophize, right under their noses the workers are poorly fed, sleep in filthy bedding, thirty or forty to a room with bedbugs everywhere and foul odors and dampness and moral corruption!

Clearly, all of our high-minded talk is just a way of deceiving ourselves and others. Tell me—where are all the nurseries they're always talking about? Where are the libraries? They're aren't any. They only exist in their vacuous little novels. What does exist is filth and ugliness and barbarity. I hate these grim faces and serious conversations—they frighten me. We'd all be better off if we'd just keep our mouths shut for a while.

Act Two. Trofimov. A field.

In this speech to Anya, Lyubov Andreevna's daughter, Trofimov uses the cherry orchard as an analogy for Russia's ignoble past and ignominious present, states that redemption will be found only in industry.

TROFIMOV

All of Russia is our orchard. Our land is vast and beautiful, and full of wonderful places. (*Pause.*) Just think of it, Anya, your grandfather, your great-grandfather—all of your ancestors—owned slaves, actually owned human souls. Look! From every cherry tree in the orchard, from every leaf, from every trunk, generations of human beings are looking at you. Listen! You can hear their voices. Owning human souls has had its effect on all of you—your ancestors living and dead! You're in debt, all of you, your mother, your uncle, even you are in debt and are living at the expense of other people; people you won't even let in your house. We're two hundred years behind the times, we've made no progress, and we don't have the slightest idea of our relation to the past. All we are are bored complainers who sit around and philosophize and drink vodka! It's clear if we're going to live in the present that we've got to first redeem our past and then put it behind us forever. And the only way we can redeem it is by suffering and committing ourselves to work—to honest, endless work! Understand, Anya?

Act One. Lopakhin. The nursery of the Ranevskaya estate.

Lopakhin had planned to meet Lyubov Andreevna at the railway station but has overslept. Here, Lopakhin, now a successful merchant, recalls his humble beginnings, Lyubov Andreevna's kindness, alludes to the fact that even though he is clad in the clothes of a wealthy man, underneath he remains a peasant.

LOPAKHIN

(*With a book in his hand.*) Of all the stupid tricks. (*He yawns and stretches.*) Coming out here so I could meet them at the station and then falling sound asleep in a chair. Stupid! (*Pause.*) Lyubov Andreevna has been living abroad for five years and I haven't got any idea what she's like now. She used to be a fine lady, kind and easygoing. I remember when I was a young fellow, about fifteen, my father, rest his soul—he ran a business in the village then—he punched me in the face and made my nose bleed. We'd come out here for some reason or other and he'd been drinking. Lyubov Andreevna, as I recall, was still very young and slim. She brought me to this very room, the nursery here, and cleaned up my face. "Don't cry, little peasant," she said, "you'll look fine at your wedding." (*Pause.*) "Little peasant." She was right, we were peasants. And still—even though I'm rich and all dressed up in a white vest and expensive boots—underneath I'm still a peasant. (*He leafs through the pages of the book.*) Like this book here. I don't understand any of it. It puts me to sleep.

Act Three. Lopakhin. A drawing room.

Lopakhin, a wealthy bourgeoisie and old family friend, has just re-turned from the auction where the cherry orchard and estate had been on the block. In a supremely ironic twist, Lopakhin reveals that it is he who purchased the entire estate, a disclosure that sends shock waves through the family and is especially devastating to Lyubov Andreevna.

LOPAKHIN

Who bought it? I did. (*There is a reaction.*) Wait! Please, my friends, give me a moment. My head's spinning, I can't talk. (*He laughs.*) It was like this—when we got to the auction, Deriganov was already there. Gayev had only fifteen thousand rubles and right off Deriganov bids thirty thousand plus what was overdue. I saw how it was going, so I jumped in and bid forty. He raised it to forty-five, and I countered with fifty-five. And so it went. He kept going up five thousand and I kept raising it by ten until, finally, I got it by bidding ninety plus what was owed. And now the cherry orchard is mine! (*He shouts with laughter.*) Good Lord, the cherry orchard is mine! Tell me I'm drunk, tell me I'm dreaming! (*He stamps his feet.*)

Don't laugh! If only my father and grandfather could rise up out of their graves and see me now: see their little Yermolay now, their ignorant little Yermolay who was always getting beaten, who ran barefoot all winter. If they could only see how I went out and just bought this estate, the most beautiful place in the world! An estate where my father and grandfather weren't even allowed in the kitchen, where they were slaves! It's all a dream, it must be! I'm asleep, I'm imagining! It can't be true! (*Smiling affectionately, he picks up the keys that had been hurled to the floor by Varya.*)

Varya threw down the keys because she knows she's no longer in charge of the house. (*He jiggles the keys.*) So, so what? (*He listens to music OFF.*) Ah! The musicians. Go ahead, musicians, play, I want to hear you! Come on everybody, come see Yermolay Lopakhin take an axe to the cherry orchard, come and see the trees come crashing down! We're going to build summer cottages, and our grandchildren and great-grandchildren are going to know a new life! Play musicians, play!

THE THREE SISTERS
(1900–1901)

Masha, Irina, and Olga are living a boring, aimless life just one year after the death of their father, who had commanded the local army post. Masha, unhappily married to a pedantic schoolteacher, involves herself in an affair with a married colonel. Olga attempts to find satisfaction in teaching, but would love to be married and have a family. Irina immerses herself in work at the local telegraph office in an attempt to avert hopelessness. The women attempt to find hope and gaiety, but it becomes evident that their efforts are futile. Their frustrations are exacerbated when their brother's bride, Natasha, a crude peasant woman, moves into the household. She slowly, deviously, gains control of the family house and disenfranchises the sisters, who are ultimately faced with leaving their homestead. Vulnerable and disillusioned, they dream of moving to Moscow, but are thwarted by impinging realities. Distressed further by the withdrawal of the army post from their city, they are obliged to face up to the hopelessness of their substitute endeavors, and accept past failures. They vow to seek again hope and direction in life.

WOMEN:

Act One. Olga. The drawing room in the Prozorov house.

In this, the play's opening speech, Olga expresses to Irina and Masha her unhappiness, her feeling of entrapment in a colorless, provincial life that is sapping her youth and vitality, her great desire for the gaiety of Moscow.

OLGA

It's been exactly one year since Father died—on your name day, Irina. It was bitter cold, snowing, remember? I didn't think I'd ever get through it. And you, you fainted dead away. But now, a year has passed and it's easier to talk about. And you're wearing white again and you look radiant. (*She listens as the clock strikes.*) The clock was striking then, too. (*Pause.*) Remember how the band was playing when they took Father to the cemetery, how they fired a graveside salute? Hardly anyone came to the funeral, and here he was, a general, a commander of the brigade. Of course, it was raining and snowing heavily at the time. (*Pause.*)

It's so warm we can have the windows open and yet there's not a single bud on the birch trees. Eleven years ago, when Father was given command of the brigade, we all came here from Moscow. I can remember perfectly the beginning of May in Moscow. By this time in Moscow everything's in full bloom, and it's warm—everything is bathed in sunlight. Eleven years have past, but I remember everything as if we'd left yesterday. Oh, dear God!

When I woke this morning and saw the sunlight everywhere, I knew right away it was springtime, and I felt my heart would burst with joy! I wanted so much to be home again. (*Pause.*) Don't whistle, Masha. How can you! (*Pause.*) After teaching high school all day every day and then giving private lessons till dinner, I have a constant headache. And my thoughts—I've even started thinking like an old woman. In fact, for the past four years I've worked at the high school, every day I've felt my strength, my youth being drained off drop by drop. Only one thing, one dream keeps me strong, keeps me going . . . Moscow!

Act Two. Natasha. The drawing room in the Prozorov house.

Natasha, a crude woman of peasant stock, has married the sisters'
brother Andrei and has bore him a son. Here, beneath a layer of
saccharinity, we discern her craftiness as she discreetly sows the
first seeds of power.

NATASHA

(*In a dressing gown, with a candle, stopping at the door leading to*
Andrei's room.) What are you doing, Andrei, reading? Oh, it's
nothing, I was just wondering . . . looking in case a light is burning.
During Carnival Week, you have to keep your eyes on the servants to
make sure nothing goes wrong. Yesterday at midnight I found a light
burning in the dining room. When I asked them who did it, I couldn't
get a straight answer. (*She puts the candle down.*)

It's a quarter past eight and Olga and Irina still aren't home. Poor
darlings, they're probably still working. Olga's at the faculty
meeting, Irina's at the telegraph office. (*She sighs.*) I told Irina this
morning, "Irina, darling," I said, "take care of yourself." But she
won't listen. I'm afraid little Bobik is sick. He's so cold. Yesterday
burning up with fever, today freezing. I'm so worried. I think it'll be
a good idea to put him on a diet. And tonight, I understand, the
maskers are coming shortly after nine. Andrei, I think it would be
better if they didn't come. When the little fellow woke this morning,
he looked at me and smiled. He recognized me. "How are you,
Bobik?" I said, "How are you, how are you?" He laughed. Children
understand. Even so, Andrei, I'll say the maskers should not be
allowed in. I know your sisters run the house, but I'll speak to them,
they'll understand. (*Going.*) The doctors say that if you're going to
lose weight, you should eat nothing but yogurt, so I've ordered you
some for dinner. (*She stops.*)

Bobik is so cold. I think he should be moved into another room till the weather's warmer. Into Irina's room, for instance—it's perfect for the baby. It's dry and sunny all day. She must be told that she has to share Olga's room for a while . . . besides, it doesn't matter, she isn't home in the daytime anyway, she's only in at night.

Act Three. Irina. Irina and Olga's room.

Natasha, the crude, cunning wife of the sisters' spineless, debt-ridden brother Andrei, has craftily insinuated herself into the household, taken over the management. Here Irina, forced to share a room with Olga, vents her bitterness and disillusionment.

IRINA

Face it: Andrei has been reduced to nothing. He has lost any depth he ever had. His energy is gone, he's become old before his time living with that woman! Once he wanted to be a professor, now he goes around bragging about being a member of the District Council. Yes, he's a member of the Council, all right, but Protopopov is the chairman—think of it! The whole town's talking about it, laughing behind his back, and he's the only one who doesn't know or see what's happening. And here he sits alone in his room, playing the violin while others are running to help out at the fire. (*Nervously.*) Oh . . . it's terrible, terrible! (*She cries.*) I—I can't stand it any longer! (*She sobs.*)

Where has it all gone? Where? God! Dear God in heaven! My head is so mixed up I can't remember anything! I can't even remember how to say "window" or "ceiling" in Italian. I'm forgetting everything! Every day I forget more and more and my life's slipping away and I'll never get it back—never! And we'll never get to Moscow . . . I know it!

(*Pulling herself together.*) I'm so unhappy! I can't work! I won't work! To hell with working, enough! I was a telegraph clerk; now I'm working at the City Council and I despise everything about it. Here I am, already twenty-three, and I've been working so long my brain's starting to go.

Look at me—thin, ugly, old . . . and nothing satisfies me, nothing. My time is slipping away and I feel like I'm moving away from a beautiful, real life into some kind of abyss. I don't have any heart anymore. I don't know why I'm still living, why I haven't killed myself by now.

MEN:

Act One. Vershinin. The drawing room in the Prozorov house.

Vershinin, a lieutenant-colonel, has a penchant for philosophizing. Here he responds to Masha's comment that they "know many useless things" by making a case for intelligence and education and the role they play in the evolution of mankind. Also, his remarks concerning the Prozorov's elegant environment lead to revelations of a wasted life, an unhappy marital situation.

VERSHININ

Well, what a funny thought. (*He laughs.*) That you know so much that is useless. You know, it's hard to imagine a place so boring and ugly that intelligent people aren't necessary. Let's say, for example, that of the hundred thousand people in this city—which is retarded and crude—that there are only three people like you. Obviously, you three people aren't going to win out over the uneducated masses around you. In fact, in your lifetime, you'll lose little by little till life devours you, till you disappear into the masses. Still, you won't vanish altogether because you will have made a beginning. After you, maybe six more like you will appear, and then twelve, and so on, until someday people like you will be the majority. Over two, three hundred years, life on the planet will be unbelievably beautiful, wonderful. Man needs intelligent life, and even though he doesn't have it yet, he must feel an intuitive need for it, and wait and dream and get ready for it, because he must see more and know more than his father and grandfather. (*He laughs.*) And you're complaining that you know too much.

(*Looking about.*) Look at all your flowers, and look at your beautiful apartment. I envy you. My whole life's been spent in cramped apartments with one couch, two chairs, and stoves that smoked all the time. This is what I've missed all my life—flowers like this. (*He rubs his hands.*) Oh well!

(*Pacing.*) I wonder sometimes—what if you had a chance to live your life all over again and knew exactly where you were going? As if your first life were just a first draft and the second time around was a final copy? I think, then, that all of us would try not to repeat ourselves and do things differently, like arrange an apartment like this for ourselves, with lots of flowers and light. I have two little girls and a wife in declining health, and so on. Well . . . if I had it all to do over again, I wouldn't get married.

Act Three. Andrei. The garden of the Prozorov house.

Andrei, the sisters' brother, was once an energetic man striving for a professional future. However, he has fallen under the influence of his crude, conniving wife, Natasha, and has taken a position on the City Council, a position arranged for him by his wife's lover, Protopopov. Now nothing more than a lethargic pawn, he bemoans his life, is repulsed by the inhabitants of the city, whom he views as evolving generations of slothful, decadent individuals.

ANDREI

Oh where is my past life, where did it go—when I was young and happy and intelligent, when I had great dreams and could think and my present and future were bright and hopeful? Why do we become dull and useless and unhappy just when we've barely started to live? Here's a town two hundred years old with over a hundred thousand people who are all exactly alike. There's never been one saint, one scholar, one artist, not a single person out of the ordinary whom anyone would want to emulate. All these people do is eat and drink and sleep, and—to beat boredom, to put a little spice in their lives—they gossip and drink and play cards and bring lawsuits. And wives deceive their husbands, and husbands keep on lying and pretend to see and hear nothing. And the children are oppressed by their parents' shallow and trivial lives, and all hope is killed in them, and—just like their fathers and mothers before them—they become tragic corpses, one identical to the other.

ORDER DIRECT

MONOLOGUES THEY HAVEN'T HEARD, Karshner. Modern speeches written in the language of today. $8.95.

MORE MONOLOGUES THEY HAVEN'T HEARD, Karshner. More exciting living-language speeches. $8.95.

SCENES THEY HAVEN'T SEEN, Karshner. Modern scenes for men and women. $7.95.

FOR WOMEN: MONOLOGUES THEY HAVEN'T HEARD, Pomerance. Contemporary speeches for actresses. $8.95

MONOLOGUES FOR KIDS, Roddy. 28 wonderful speeches for boys and girls. $8.95.

MORE MONOLOGUES for KIDS, Roddy. More great speeches for boys and girls. $8.95.

SCENES for KIDS, Roddy. 30 scenes for girls and boys. $8.95.

MONOLOGUES for TEENAGERS, Karshner. Contemporary teen speeches. $8.95.

SCENES for TEENAGERS, Karshner. Scenes for today's teen boys and girls. $7.95.

HIGH-SCHOOL MONOLOGUES THEY HAVEN'T HEARD, Karshner. Contemporary speeches for high-schoolers, $7.95.

DOWN-HOME, Karshner. Great character speeches for men and women in the language of rural America. $7.95.

MONOLOGUES from the CLASSICS, ed. Karshner. Speeches from Shakespeare, Marlowe, and others. An excellent collection for men and women, $7.95.

SCENES from the CLASSICS, ed. Maag. Scenes from Shakespeare and others. $7.95.

SHAKESPEARE'S MONOLOGUES THEY HAVEN'T HEARD, ed. Dotterer. Lesser-known speeches from The Bard. $7.95.

MONOLOGUES from CHEKHOV, trans. Cartwright. Modern translations from Chekhov's major plays: *Cherry Orchard, Uncle Vanya, Three Sisters, The Sea gull.* $8.95.

MONOLOGUES from GEORGE BERNARD SHAW, ed. Michaels. Great speeches for men and women from the works of G.B.S. $7.95.

MONOLOGUES from OSCAR WILDE, ed. Michaels. The best of Wilde's urbane, dramatic writing from his greatest plays. For men and women. $7.95.

WOMAN, Pomerance. Monologues for actresses. $8.95.

MODERN SCENES for WOMEN, Pomerance. Scenes for today's actresses. $7.95.

MONOLOGUES from MOLIÈRE, trans. Dotterer. A definitive collection of speeches from the French Master. The first translation into English prose. $9.95.

SHAKESPEARE'S MONOLOGUES for WOMEN, ed. Dotterer. $8.95.

DIALECT MONOLOGUES, Karshner/Stern. 13 essential dialects applied to contemporary monologues. Book and cassette tape. $19.95.

YOU SAID a MOUTHFUL, Karshner. Tongue twisters galore. Great exercises for actors, singers, public speakers. Fun for everyone. $7.95.

TEENAGE MOUTH, Karshner. Modern monologues for young men and women. $8.95.

SHAKESPEARE'S LADIES, ed. Dtterer. A second book of Shakespeare's monologues for women. With a descriptive text on acting Shakespeare. $7.95.

BETH HENLEY: MONOLOGUES FOR WOMEN, Henley. *Crimes of the Heart*, others. $7.95.

CITY WOMEN, Smith. 20 powerful, urban monologues. Great audition pieces. $7.95.

KIDS' STUFF, Roddy. 30 great audition pieces for children. $7.95.

KNAVES, KNIGHTS, AND KINGS, ed. Dotterer. Shakespeare's speeches for men. $8.95.

DIALECT MONOLOGUES, VOL. II, Karshner/Stern. 14 more important dialects. Farsi, Afrikaans, Asian Indian, etc. Book and cassette tape. $19.95.

RED LICORICE, Tippit. 31 great scene-monologues for preteens. $8.95.

MODERN MONOLOGUES FOR MODERN KIDS, Mauro. $7.95.

A WOMAN SPEAKS: WOMEN FAMOUS, INFAMOUS and UNKNOWN, ed. Cosentino. $12.95.

FITTING IN, Mauro. Modern monoloues for boys and girls. $8.95.

VOICES, ed. Cosentino. Scene-study pieces for women. $12.95.

FOR WOMEN: MORE MONOLOGUES THEY HAVEN'T HEARD, Pomerance. $8.95

Send your check or money order (no cash or COD) plus handling charges of $4.00 for the first book and $1.50 for each additional book. California residents add 8.25 % tax. Send your order to: Dramaline Publications, 36-851 Palm View Road, Rancho Mirage, California 92270.